Don't Behave Like You Live in a Cave

by Elizabeth Verdick

Illustrated by Steve Mark

free spirit
PUBLISHING®

Library of Congress Cataloging-in-Publication Data
Verdick, Elizabeth.
   Don't behave like you live in a cave / by Elizabeth Verdick.
      p. cm.—(Laugh & learn series)
   Includes index.
   ISBN 978-1-57542-353-1
1. Child psychology—Juvenile literature. 2. Children—Conduct of life—Juvenile literature.
3. Etiquette for children and teenagers—Juvenile literature. I. Title.
   HQ772.5.V47 2010
   395.1'22—dc22

                                                    2010010441

Free Spirit Publishing does not have control over, or assume responsibility for, author or third-party Web sites and their content. At the time of this book's publication, all facts and figures cited within are the most current available. All telephone numbers, addresses, and Web site URLs are accurate and active; all publications, organizations, Web sites, and other resources exist as described in this book; and all have been verified as of April 2010. If you find an error or believe that a resource listed here is not as described, please contact Free Spirit Publishing. Parents, teachers, and other adults: We strongly urge you to monitor children's use of the Internet.

Reading Level Grades 4–5; Interest Level Ages 8–13;
Fountas & Pinnell Guided Reading Level T

Edited by Eric Braun
Designed by Michelle Lee
Cover wallpaper pattern ©istockphoto.com/BOOJOO

10 9 8 7 6 5 4 3 2 1
Printed in Hong Kong
P17200610

Free Spirit Publishing Inc.
217 Fifth Avenue North, Suite 200
Minneapolis, MN 55401-1299
(612) 338-2068
help4kids@freespirit.com
www.freespirit.com

Dedication

For Zach: My sweet boy, who works hard even when his days are hard, and brightens my days with his made-up, one-of-a-kind jokes.

Acknowledgments

Sincere thanks to Jennifer Salava, Ed.S., NCSP, for her expertise as this book was being developed.

Contents

Oh, Behave!

- Do other kids often give you the "What is *up* with *you*" look?

- Do people ever ask, "Were you born in a BARN?"

- Do adults say you "act up" or "act out"?

- Do they yell, "Why do you act like this?!" while pulling out their hair?

Maybe you tell them:

It's no "act."
It's just how I am!
I can't HELP it!

And maybe you secretly wonder:

Am I, like, a
PROBLEM CHILD?

Well, no. You're a great kid in many, many ways. But maybe you need to make smarter choices about how you behave at home and school. Why? So . . .

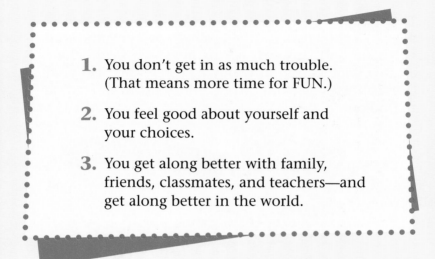

1. You don't get in as much trouble. (That means more time for FUN.)

2. You feel good about yourself and your choices.

3. You get along better with family, friends, classmates, and teachers—and get along better in the world.

You wouldn't be the first kid who needs this kind of help, and you won't be the last. *Lots* of people have difficulty with their behavior at some point in life, for different reasons—adults included. You're not alone!

Chapter 1
What's the Big Deal?

This book isn't about turning you into a "perfect" person, a goody-goody, the teacher's pet, or some kind of **robot-kid.** Instead, it can help you take a look at how you act and how other people *react*. Do your actions help you—or do they hurt you? Keep reading to find out.

A Really Stupid Story

"There," said Cave Girl. "I'm all ready."

Cave Boy took one look at her and burst out laughing. *What was she wearing?* Her new animal-hide outfit looked stupid.

If there was one thing Cave Girl couldn't stand, it was people laughing at her. She screamed "Wedgie!" and gave Cave Boy's loincloth a yank.

Bang, bang, bang! Their cave-guests were at the cave-door. Soon they were all seated around a big stone table, their wooden clubs resting nearby. Cave Boy plunked down a plate of delicious cooked meat and said, "Dig in."

Cave Girl grabbed the biggest piece and stuffed her face. Cave Boy started laughing at her again.

"Cave Girl," he said, "you eat like a *Daeodon*."*

"Are you calling me a stinky old hog?" she asked. She tossed the meat bone in the corner and glared.

"What if I am?" said Cave Boy.

Cave Girl lifted her club. "Shut up, or I'll smash you!"

"I'll smash you right back!" He grabbed his club.

The other cave-kids kept eating. That meat was really good.

Cave Boy and Cave Girl jumped up from the table, clubs raised. They chased each other out the door, yelling threats at the top of their lungs.

* A giant, monstrous prehistoric pig

No one in the cave made a move to stop them because, to be honest, things were easier without those two around.

Cave Girl and Cave Boy were so busy yelling insults at each other that they didn't notice BIG trouble just around the corner . . .

The End
(in more ways than one)

Quick Quiz

And the moral of that cave story is?

(A) Watch out for hungry saber-toothed tigers.

(B) Get yourself a really big club.

(C) Don't behave like you live in a cave.

Answer: C. Easiest quiz ever.

What do Cave Boy and Cave Girl have to do with a modern kid like you? Glad you asked.

Cave Girl was big on wedgies and hitting people with her club. Cave Boy was always taunting people and making a pest of himself. What can you expect? They were Cave Kids—they hadn't evolved much.

You, on the other hand, are evolving quite nicely. But, like any kid, you sometimes do things that make adults go ARRRRGH! Soon, they're watching your every move (like hungry saber-toothed tigers). You don't need *that.*

You want the people in your life—grown-ups and kids alike—to look at you and think, "That is one cool kid." Right?

Right.

Young man, your behavior is inappropriate!

Sound Familiar?

Uh-oh. You got caught doing something you weren't supposed to do.

Or, you got caught *not* doing something you *were* supposed to do. Either way, it's trouble.

Trouble-makers

Aw, I was just messing around.

Using a whoopee cushion in class

Toilet-papering someone's house

Imitating the teacher

Writing rude jokes on the bathroom wall

Tripping kids in the hall

Farting on your sister

Making your brother eat a bug

Teasing someone in a mean way, then saying "Just kidding"

Making prank phone calls

Inappropriate is a big word used to describe a bunch of different behaviors—some worse than others. Looking at the lists on pages 9 and 10, you can probably guess that hitting will lead to more trouble than teasing or blowing off a chore. But what if some of the things on the list seem "harmless" to you? Like, is it really *so* bad to fart on people or tell your parents their meatloaf tastes like barf?

It's true that "bad" behaviors can range from mildly annoying to **YOU'RE GONNA BE SORRY YOU DID THAT.** Some of them hurt others. But no matter how big or small the behaviors may be, they're getting you something called *negative attention.*

Negative attention focuses on what you do wrong, or on what people think you *might* do wrong. That means a lot of:

Negative attention can come in the form of corrections, threats, and punishments. After a while, you might be so used to that kind of attention you almost forget about the other kind: *positive attention.*

What does **positive attention** look like?

a smile

a thank you

praise

high fives hugs

compliments

pats on the back

At least, that's what positive attention looks like on the outside. Inside, positive attention can look like pride, confidence, and self-respect.

Throughout this book, you'll learn positive ways to behave. Positive *behavior* often leads to positive *attention,* which then leads to positive *feelings* inside.

a positive + a positive = a POSITIVE

Positive attention feels great. Pretty soon, friends might want to spend more time with you. Classmates might notice the *good* things you do. Younger kids might look up to you. Even your cat might start to think you're as cool as canned sardines.

Plus, the adults in your life (maybe the one who handed you this book) will have warm-and-fuzzy thoughts like, "What a *delightful* young man" or "That girl is a real peach."

Most importantly: You'll feel good about YOU.

Help!

All this talk about behavior and cave kids can get confusing. What if . . .

- you're not sure how your family and teachers expect you to act?

- you have trouble understanding behavior rules?

- you forget the rules or don't care much about them?

- you feel like your body, brain, or feelings get out of control?

- you seem to hear more about what you're doing "wrong" than what you're doing *right?*

Those what-ifs are big challenges, the kind that are hard to tackle on your own. Anytime you face a big challenge, you need someone you can count on— someone who's on your side. Think of the adults (or at least one adult) you trust most. How about:

- a parent or close relative

- your teacher

- your school's guidance counselor (or another specialist at school)

- the school principal

- your doctor or a therapist (an adult trained to help you with your feelings, behaviors, skills, or relationships with other people)

The person you choose can show you which behaviors help you and which ones hurt you. He or she can be your resource for setting behavior goals and reaching them.

So if you can, go ask that person now. The book can wait. Is now not a good time? Maybe the person isn't around, or he or she is busy now. If that's the case, make a plan to talk to that adult later—then follow through with your plan.

You might say:

66 I'm having trouble handling things at school/home. I know there are some behaviors I need to change—but I don't know where to start. Can you help me? 99

1. You can read this book with the adult. Or,

2. You can read it on your own but get a trusted grown-up's help when it's time to think about your behaviors. Whenever you see:

you'll know an adult is needed.

P.S. Maybe grown-ups have said you *have* to talk to someone about this stuff. If so, that's okay because they want what's best for you. Talking about feelings and problems *helps*—give it a chance.

P.P.S. Sometimes parents have problems, too. They might need to get expert help before they can be there for you. You can look to other people for help: a grandparent, another relative who lives nearby, or your teacher.

Chapter 2
Let's Get Going

Here you are, at the starting line. You're pumped. You're ready. You have a coach. (Right? A coach—an adult helper—you found one, didn't you?)

Now you're headed in the right direction.

All you have to do is start to walk the line.

Walking the Line

Your two feet go here.

Walk, walk, one foot in front of the other—so easy a cave kid can do it.

But for the purposes of this book, there's more to walking the line than just walking. Think of the line as a divider. It separates above-the-line behavior (the appropriate kind) from below-the-line behavior (the inappropriate kind). You want to walk on the **above** side of the line. For example . . .

Above the Line

- ★ Paying attention in class
- ★ Doing chores
- ★ Being kind to others
- ★ Doing homework
- ★ Staying calm

Below the Line

- ★ Goofing off in class
- ★ Refusing to do chores
- ★ Being mean to others
- ★ Blowing off homework
- ★ Blowing up at someone

When you walk above the line, you stay on a good path. You focus on helpful behaviors, and you steer clear of hurtful ones.

Hit the Pause Button for a Sec

Take a moment to think about that: Some behaviors *help* and others *hurt.*

Well, how are you supposed to tell the difference?

Try the old sniff test. You should smell trouble if you're . . .

- trying to get away with something you know is wrong

- doing something you've been told *not* to do

- hurting someone's body or feelings

- getting negative attention

- feeling bad about what you do

- the *only* one laughing

Makin' a List, Checkin' It Twice

Get a piece of paper and a pencil so you can draw your own line. Think of some things you already do that are above the line. Like, helping your sister with her homework, taking out the trash, or sharing stuff with friends. List them—and make the list as long as you want. You can even make two lists: one that focuses on things you do at home, and the other on things you do at school.

Above the Line (Home)

Clearing the table
Emailing Grandma
Eating my vegetables at dinner
Giving the dog belly rubs
Helping Dad wash the car
Telling the truth

A list like this helps you see the many things you're doing well. Add to it as often as you'd like.

Now think about some of your behaviors that are below the line. (Maybe you blurt out a lot in class, boss your brother around, talk back to your parents, or pick fights with kids at school.) **Don't worry:** The idea here is NOT to list everything you've ever done wrong or to come up with tons of behaviors you need to improve. Keep it simple. See if you and your adult helper can think of three behaviors that make it harder for you to have good days at school or at home. Example:

Below the Line (Home)

Refusing to do my homework, or blowing it off

Yelling at Mom

Not getting out of bed when my alarm goes off

Changing a behavior takes *PRACTICE*—lots of it. The key is to replace each negative behavior with a *POSITIVE* one. Just think **PP.** Good old **PP.** You can remember that, can't you?

Simple Steps to Start

Suppose you decide to work on the "Refusing to do homework, or blowing it off" behavior (from the sample list on page 22). Here are five steps you can take:

1. **Change the negative to a positive.** Say what you *will* do, instead of what you won't do.

> "I will do my homework each day after school and one day on the weekend."

2. **Write it down.** On a calendar or planner, write what you need to do every day. Example:

Day	What I need to do...
Monday	Do homework before dinner.
Tuesday	Do homework after soccer practice.
Wednesday	Study spelling words right after school (test Thursday).
Thursday	Finish all homework before dinner.
Friday	Take it easy!
Saturday	Do all homework before hanging out with friends.
Sunday	Ahhh, time off.

Once you've done what you need to do each day, give yourself a checkmark or star. The checks/stars could even lead to rewards. (For more on that, see Chapter 6.)

3. **Get some support.** Tell your adult helper about what you're trying to accomplish. That person can give you reminders, suggestions, and high fives.

4. **Give yourself a hand.** Some days you're going to do what you set out to do—and that's great! You'll probably feel energized and proud. You may want to write about the good feelings so you remember them.

5. **Give yourself a break.** Other days, you may get busy and forget about the change you're trying to make, or you might be in a bad mood and not get to your task. That's okay. No need to beat yourself up over it. Just tell yourself to get back on track the next day—and keep going.

Who Needs to Know?

You're working on your behavior—and starting to make changes in your life. That's not easy to do! It takes time, practice, and persistence (meaning you stick with it).

Does the whole world have to know? That's up to you. If you decide to tell your friends and other kids what you're working on, that's okay. On the other hand, you may want to keep the information to yourself—no problem there. You don't have to go around carrying a big sign that says:

Tell your parents and your teacher that you want to keep things private. Together, you can make some **secret signals** for times when an adult needs to remind you to behave a different way.

The signal should be something simple that doesn't draw other people's attention but tells *you* exactly what you need to know. It could be a hand gesture, a touch on the shoulder, or a note that's passed to you with a quick reminder. Practice the signal together to make sure it works.

Chapter 3
Rules Rule (yeah, Right)

If you think . . .

. . . then try saying *that* five times fast.

It's true that schools have lots of rules, and rules are tools . . . and pools are cool. But the important thing about rules is this: Rules exist so people have a clue what to do. Can you imagine if there were no rules of the road, and drivers could go where they wanted, when they wanted, as fast as they wanted?

At school, having rules about what students can and can't do makes the day go smoother for everyone. Otherwise, school might look something like this:

Most schools have a handbook or handout that tells students (and their parents) what the rules are. Take a look and you're likely to see rules about not . . .

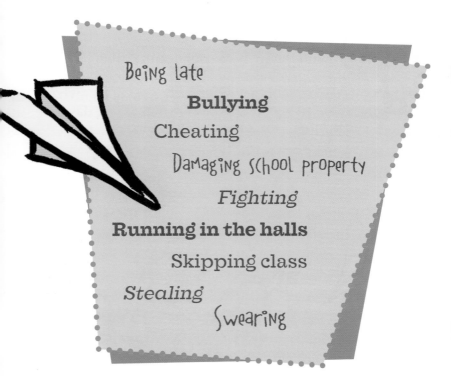

Being late

Bullying

Cheating

Damaging school property

Fighting

Running in the halls

Skipping class

Stealing

Swearing

Why follow the rules? Because you'll get along better with your teachers and other students. You'll spend less time in the principal's office or detention room. And you'll learn more, which helps make you smarter and more confident.

Rules are about *rights*. You—and the other students—have a right to go to a school where you're safe and where students respect each other, the teachers, and school property.

If you're known around school as someone who breaks or bends the rules, that's going to make it harder for you to do well in class and get along with other people. The confusing thing is that breaking rules tends to get you attention—maybe other kids laugh or they watch to see what you'll do next. They might think of you as cool, funny, or tough, and that gets you noticed.

The risky thing is that it's *negative* attention people are giving you (read more about that on page 11). Over time, you might start to believe that trouble-making is a part of who you are and so you keep it up . . . forgetting that things don't actually have to be this way.

If your behavior at school gets you noticed in a not-so-good way, you can help yourself by keeping a **trouble tracker.** In a notebook, write down when you get in trouble at school and why it happened.

Ms. McGhee told me three times not to fiddle with my pencil.

Got caught passing notes in science.

Jessie told me to quit pushing and annoying people in line.

The principal saw me wearing a T-shirt that broke the rules (made me put on a sweatshirt over it).

Bus driver told me to keep my voice down.

Keep the list going for a week. Afterward, look it over. How many times did an adult talk to you about your behavior? What about other students—did they say stuff to you, too? (How did you feel about that?)

Think about what's going on with you at school. Do you forget the rules? Do you get bored? Do you think people won't notice if you're doing something you're not supposed to do? Are certain subjects or classes more difficult for you—and you're frustrated? Does it seem as if your teacher is too strict with you? Do you clown around to get other kids to notice you or try to make them laugh?

AN ADULT CAN HELP YOU HERE

Share the trouble tracker with an adult you trust. Talk about ways you could change your behavior for the better. Then go back to the sections called "Walking the Line" (page 18) and "Simple Steps to Start" (page 23). Choose one behavior to work on at school for a week or two.

For example, maybe the school library is a place where you're always getting *shushed*. Make a goal like "Library time is my quiet time." Have a plan before you go, like knowing which section or shelf you want to visit or which book(s) you want to check out. Walk quietly instead of rushing around. If standing in line and waiting is a problem for you, use that time to get started on your reading so you won't be tempted to talk. Or recite something in your head: your favorite movies, NFL teams, president names, the times tables. And remember, *Shhhhh.*

Family Rules

Do you know the rules at home? Do you *remember* them? Do you FOLLOW them? If your answers are: "Sort of," "Sometimes," or "When I feel like it," then your home might be a stress mess. Not just for you but for everyone in the family, even the dog.

In any community (like a family), people have to agree on ways to live together and get along. Unless you're Cave Girl or Cave Boy, you can't just go around grunting and knocking people on the head with a club.

Talk to your dad or mom about the rules at home. Write them down and post them where everyone can see them.

> **Tip:** Wording the rules positively can be positively brilliant—then people focus on what *to* do, instead of what *not* to do.

You might try "Use a calm voice" instead of *No screaming and yelling!*

No hitting! becomes "Keep your hands to yourself."

Hey, it just sounds better that way.

At home, your family can work on giving each other FRIENDLY reminders if somebody forgets the rules:

"I just heard you cussing, and one of our rules is not to swear. It's just nicer around here when people remember that, okay?"

Moment of truth: There may be times when you don't follow a rule, no one sees, and you get away with it. It's not like you have a hidden camera following your every move! So, does it matter if you break the rules but don't get caught?

Well, *you* know what you did (or didn't do). Deep down, you know that your words or your actions didn't match up with your family's expectations. That can be a stressful feeling. How can you make things right again?

 Admit what happened.

 Give yourself a "do-over" (a chance to try again).

 Remember to follow the rule next time.

Rules can be hard to remember. So, if there's any doubt in your mind about what you're *supposed* to be doing and *why,* just remember one very simple rule . . .

The Golden Rule: Treat others the way YOU want to be treated.

You can even take the Golden Rule one step further:

Treat other people's stuff the way you want YOUR stuff to be treated.

If you remember the Golden Rule at home, at school, and anywhere else you go in life, you'll stay above the line you're trying to walk. (See page 18.)

Chapter 4
Five Great Goals for Better Behavior (5GG4BB)

Athletes practice their skills a lot. They do warm-ups, stretches, and drills. If they didn't keep in shape this way, they wouldn't get too far in their sport.

Like an athlete, you can build your skills—*life* skills—every day, bit by bit, to get along better in the world. Working on **5GG4BB** makes you a stronger person. You'll gain more confidence about what you say and do each day. You'll feel more positive about yourself, your family, and school.

By the way, athletes need people rooting for them. So do you. Ask your family or friends for support.

Goal #1 Listen Up

Does your school day ever look a little something like this?

What your teacher says:

Even though there's no school tomorrow, I'm giving you some challenging homework. It's due after our day off. We'll see how you do, and good luck!

What you hear:

Blah blah blah, la la la, **NO** blah blah, la la, homework. See you!

You think:

Cool! No homework!

Maybe when teachers or parents start talking, you start to:

* Daydream
* Stare at the clock
* Sort of listen, but not really

* Roll your eyes and sigh
* Talk to someone else
* Tune out
* Drift off . . . *ZZZzzzzz*

Wake up!
Listening is a big part of doing well in school and in life. Maybe you weren't born a good listener— but you can train yourself to become one.

Huh? What? Slick Tricks for Power-Steering Your Hearing

Use your eyes as well as your ears. Look at the person who's talking. Watch their lips or look them in the eye. This helps you stay in the moment and pay closer attention.

Take notes. Write down what you hear the person say. (That may seem weird to do at home, especially when Dad is giving you another lecture on how to sort your socks, but notes *can* help you remember.) You don't have to write every single word—just the ones that will remind you what's important.

Repeat what you heard. Suppose your teacher says, "Do problems 1–20 on pages 45–47 of the textbook." Maybe you didn't catch all that the first time. You can raise your hand and ask, "Did you say to do problems 1–20? I just want to be sure I heard what you said." Sometimes you need to hear something twice before it sinks in.

Check for distractions. Is something getting in the way of your listening? Are other kids talking? Is there background noise (like a TV or radio you could turn off)? Are you hungry, thirsty, tired, or fidgety? Do you have a problem you're not sure how to handle? To clear your head, take a few deep breaths in and out. Get some oxygen to your brain so you can pay attention to what you need to hear. (See pages 94–97 for more on how something as simple as breathing can help.)

Don't try to do everything at once. Maybe it's hard for you to listen to someone, and write something down, *and* read the board, AND stay still in your seat, all at the same time. Talk to a parent or your teacher about finding ways to slow down each task so you can give it your full attention. Not everyone can "multi-task" well—you may need extra practice.

Tell yourself "Ears open, mouth shut." Take a closer look at what's going on when you're supposed to be listening. Do you talk to others? Blurt out answers? Interrupt? Make wisecracks? If your lips are moving, you're probably not listening as well as you could.

Remember . . .

Adults *like* it when you listen. It makes them feel heard, even if you really think they're clueless.

 If you listen harder at school, you'll learn more, you'll have a better idea of what to do, and your teacher will be more likely to think of you as a good student, which can lead to nice comments on your report card like, "Thor is a joy to have in class."

 If you listen more at home, your mom or dad will probably notice and feel better about your behavior. That means less stress at home.

How to Look Like You're Listening at School

Since you're working so hard at listening,
be sure to *look*
like you're
listening, too.

☑ Keep your eyes focused on your teacher and the board.

☑ Smile, or at least look interested.

☑ Make sure your mouth isn't moving.

☑ Nod your head to show you understand.

☑ Raise your hand if you have a question or an idea.

☑ Wait to be called on.

☑ Use *polite* words for questions or comments . . .

For example, try:

> 66 Some of this is confusing me. Can you say that part again, please? 99

Not:

> 66 Could this BE any more boring?! What's the point? 99

 Looking like you're listening naturally leads to . . . listening. So, you not only satisfy your teacher but also actually get the info you need.

Goal #2 Just Do It

Do you go around yelling stuff like:

Everybody's always telling me what to do!

And then, in the very next breath, do you say something like:

I wish I had my own place so I could do whatever I want and take care of mySELF!

Followed by:

Mom, I'm hungry, can you make me a bologna sandwich?

The fact is, you're still a kid. That has its ups and downs.

One nice perk of being a kid is that your dad, mom, or some other adult is there to make sure you have clothes, food, and a place to live. It's a grown-up's job to see that you're safe and to help you grow up to be the best person you can be. As a kid, it's your job to try to follow the rules and do what your parents ask you to do. Sure, it's not always fun—especially if you get stuck scrubbing the toilet or scooping cat poop.

There's good news, though. Someday you'll be an adult, and then *you* can tell kids what to do. You can shake your knobby old cane and shout:

IN My day, we did what we were told, and we LIKED it, you lazy little whippersnappers!

So, what's all this leading up to? A very simple question: Do you do what you're told?

If your mom says, "I need you to wash the dishes," do you say, "Sure thing, Ma"?

Or, is it more like:

> 66 What? The *dishes?* They have *crud* on them! No fair! Why do *I* have to do *everything?* Why is it always me, me, *ME?* You're ruining my life!!! 99

And if your teacher says, "Please come up and do this math problem on the board," do you say, "Okay, it looks like a hard one but I'll give it a shot"?

Or do you:

Say "What*ever*," roll your eyes, slump, sigh, walk to the board s-l-o-w-l-y, grab the marker, drop the marker, sigh again, roll your eyes and slump again, and generally make it known that you have way better things to do with your time?

The truth is you're probably going to end up doing the job anyway, even if you raise a big stink. Whining and complaining take a lot of effort and energy. Why not put the effort and energy into getting the task done? You just *do* it, it's done, you've made an adult happy, and you're out of there. (Hey, you'll be happy, too.)

How to Do What You Don't Want to Do

☑ Think about how good you'll feel when you're finished, not how awful it will be to do it.

☑ Ask yourself, "What will happen if I get it done?" Then ask yourself, "What will happen to me if I *don't* get it done?" (Maybe you'll get in trouble?)

☑ To help motivate yourself to get started, decide to do the task for just five minutes. Set a timer and start. When the timer goes off, stop. If you're not done, come back after a short break and start that timer up again.

☑ For longer jobs, like cleaning a really messy room, take frequent breaks (10 to 15 minutes at the most). During your breaks, do something that gives you energy like dancing, running, throwing a ball, or walking your dog.

☑ Play music while doing the task—or sing, tell knock-knock jokes, or do whatever else keeps your mind busy while your hands do the work.

☑ While you're doing the task, focus on what you've already completed—at least you've gotten that far! Now keep going . . . don't give up!

☑ Play beat-the-clock. Estimate how long it will take you to get the job done. Just a few minutes? Less than a half hour? More? Now set a timer and race to see if you can beat your estimated time. *Tip:* Be sure you still get the job done *well,* instead of skipping a bunch of steps to get it done fast.

☑ Ask for help. Maybe the job is hard. Maybe it's boring. Would it be easier and more fun if you had a helper? Ask a friend or a sibling to give you a hand. You can offer to do something for him or her in return.

☑ Let an adult know if you're stuck. Maybe you don't know HOW to do the job. Do you need help getting started? Do you need advice about what steps to take? Do you sometimes get lost or frustrated? It's okay to need help! An adult can help you get started, keep going, *and* finish up.

The great thing about getting something done is that it gives you a sense of "I did it!" Who doesn't like *that* feeling? Even if you're tired afterward, you might get a little jolt of energy thinking, "I'm done, and I rock."

Goal #3 Stop, Think, Go

Put yourself in this kid's place:

CRASH!!!

What might your reaction be?

(A) You scream, "You #@*#! You ruined my project! You are SO going to get it!"

(B) Your fists start flying, and you're going to kick some major butt no matter how much trouble you'll get in.

(C) You stomp on the remaining pieces of your diorama, because you might as well wreck the whole dumb thing.

(D) You burst into tears, run for the bathroom, slam the stall door, and refuse to ever come out again.

Answer: None of the above—because you can smell a trick quiz a mile away.

Here's a true, unavoidable fact of life: Stuff happens. We all have tough times we have to get through. Some of the stuff that happens to you might leave you feeling bummed out, sad, confused, irritated, angry, or completely furious. When stuff happens, you need a plan. This plan should be simple enough that you can remember it and use it even in situations that upset you a lot.

You know what's simple? A traffic light. **RED** for stop, **YELLOW** for caution, and **GREEN** for go. Your plan can be as basic as **STOP THINK GO**.

As soon as you start to have strong feelings you aren't sure how to handle, STOP. Putting on the brakes is important so you won't do something to make the situation worse.

THINK a moment before you do anything. Take a few deep, calming breaths. What's the best way to handle the situation? This isn't a time to get physical (hitting, punching) or say something that will be hard to take back.

Ask yourself:

What do I need to do to stay calm?

What can I do that will HELP the situation?

How do I avoid doing something that might HURT me or somebody else?

Do I need an adult's help here?

Next, GO ahead and act—give your *best* response, based on the questions you've asked yourself. Be sure to choose an action that *helps*—one that won't get you into trouble or make things worse.

Dealing with the Diorama Dilemma

So your diorama went splat. What next? Here are some ways to **STOP** **THINK** **GO:**

STOP

Put on those brakes—keep your hands, feet, and words to yourself. Take a look at the situation. You might start crying—it's okay, that happens. Just focus on staying as calm and cool as you can, instead of yelling.

THINK

Consider what happened . . . it probably was an accident that someone ran into you, and that person probably feels sorry.

What do I need to do to stay calm?
I can take deep breaths.

What can I do that will HELP the situation?
I can start picking up the pieces.

How do I avoid doing something that might HURT me or somebody else?
Instead of thinking about how sad or mad I am, I can focus on cleaning up. I can tell myself to remain calm. If the other person tries to apologize, I can listen.

Do I need an adult's help here? I can get my teacher and show him what happened. I can ask for extra time to repair my project.

GO
Your project got messed up, but it can be fixed. You could say to the person who ran into you: "I know it was an accident. Can you help me pick up this stuff?" If the person says sorry, be forgiving. Accept the apology and move on.

Remember . . .
It's okay to get angry, but avoid going all "Neanderthal" on everyone. Put down that club, and don't get your loincloth in a tangle.

Hee Hee

Pay attention to your body's *anger warning signs:*

- Do you feel like you're getting hotter, like blood is rushing to your ears and face?

- Do you feel shaky, jumpy, or ready to burst?

- Are your thoughts spinning out of control?

- Does your stomach or your head hurt?

- Are your hands squeezed into fists?

These are signs to **STOP.** Sometimes, that's hard to do! If you have a temper and you're used to screaming and yelling, then stopping yourself is tough—but *really* important. Keep practicing, and over time you'll get better at it.

As you **STOP,** take some deep breaths. **THINK** before you do anything. **GO** only *after* you've started to calm down.

On pages 94–97, you'll find some breathing exercises that can help you chill out when your temper heats up.

Goal #4 **Own Up**

Do any of these sound familiar?

Excuses, excuses.

Sometimes, do you blame others for the things you've done instead of taking responsibility for your actions? Well, here's a little secret: Everyone does that. *Adults* do that. Even the kindest, most peaceful people on the planet sometimes do that. We can all work a little harder to do it less.

Next time you start placing blame or saying stuff like . . .

※ ※ "I didN't do it. It wasN't my fault. I mean, ※ ※
※ ※ it wouldN't have been my fault if I'd done ※ ※
※ ※ something, but I didN't DO anything, so it's ※ ※
※ ※ not my fault!" ※ ※

. . . stop and own up. Take responsibility for what you did.

You might say:

"Yeah, I made a mistake."

OR:

"It was my fault."

An apology might be needed. So say:

"I'm sorry, I really am."

OR:

"I apologize. Can you forgive me?"

OR:

"I feel bad that I did that, and I won't let it happen again."

If you mess up, 'fess up!

Taking responsibility for your behavior is a big deal—a really BIG DEAL. It shows that you're learning from your experiences and from your mistakes.

Sometimes, it might feel weird to say, "I made a mistake," or "I goofed that up, didn't I?" (Especially if in the past you've made a lot of excuses for your behavior.) It takes courage to admit that you're wrong or that you've made a poor choice—and your courage counts for something. It's a sign that you're changing your ways and growing up.

P.S. When adults see you taking responsibility for your actions, they're probably going to think stuff like, "Gosh, Clarabelle sure is making an effort. She's SO *responsible* now. Let's give her some more independence—we can trust her more than we used to."

Totally worth it!

Goal #5 Tell It Like It Is

It can be so embarrassing when you're caught in a lie. You might try to cover it up with a bunch more lies, like:

Lying is like sinking in quicksand—the more you struggle, the worse the situation gets. Glub, glub.

Why do people lie?

Maybe they think the lie sounds more impressive than the truth.

Maybe they don't want to get in trouble for something they did.

Or maybe they're covering up for someone else.

At times, the truth is just *hard.* What if you don't want to be friends with someone anymore, for example? It may seem easier to make up lies like, "I'm super busy so I can't hang out," or "I have a really rare, contagious disease—so it's better if you stay away from me for a while."

The truth is, most people eventually get caught in their own web of lies, like flies.

Lying is one of those below-the-line behaviors (for more on those, see pages 18–19) that gets you in trouble at home and at school. Avoiding trouble is a good reason not to lie. But there's an even better reason: BEING TRUE TO YOURSELF. When you tell lies and people believe them, you may have fooled *them* but you're not fooling yourself. Deep down, you know you lied. That knowledge can leave you feeling like a fake, or feeling worried and upset. Being truthful, on the other hand, feels real. Because it's the real deal.

BUT . . . (and this is a really BIG but) . . .

If your mom comes home with a hideous new hairdo, you don't have to tell her she looks like she got attacked by a weed-whacker. Just say, "Hey, that's a new look for you—how do you like it?" That's not a lie—you're still being *honest* but in a way that won't hurt someone's feelings.

In other words, just because you *think* something doesn't mean you have to SAY it, even if it's true.

From time to time, you might think thoughts that could be hurtful—but you don't have to say them. You really, really don't need to tell your buddy that your *dog* could write a better song.

Let your rather-rude-but-perfectly-honest thought stay in its thought bubble.

AND DON'T POP THAT BUBBLE!

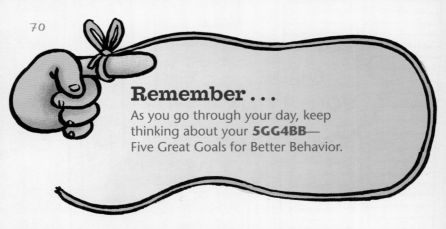

Remember . . .

As you go through your day, keep thinking about your **5GG4BB**—Five Great Goals for Better Behavior.

1. When you wake up in the morning, remind yourself to practice your goals that day.

2. Focus on your goals while you're at school and talk about them again at home.

3. Keep notes on your calendar or in your planner so you stay focused—or use a behavior chart to keep track (there's a sample chart on page 109).

4. You can also give yourself little pep talks before bed, like: "I'm proud of myself that I'm working on my behavior goals."

Another good time to remember your goals is when you're *on the move:*

 When you walk in the front door (home, school, or anywhere)

 On the school bus or waiting at the bus stop

 In the school hallways and in line

 When you enter the classroom

 On the playground

 When you go to other places in your school: the gym, water fountain, resource room, cafeteria, media center, bathroom, the music or art room, and so on

You can continue putting your best foot forward by remembering to do a few more simple things each day:

☑ **Smile.** (See how nice you look?)

☑ **Scrub-a-dub-dub.** You'll look and feel better if you bathe or shower more frequently as you head on your way toward puberty.

☑ **Wear it well.** No, you don't have to dress to impress—who cares what labels you wear or what store you get your clothes from? As long as your clothes are clean (don't pull them out of the hamper), you tuck in your shirt once in a while, and your underwear isn't showing, that's a good start.

☑ **Be confident in who you are.** Don't let other people make you think less of yourself. Find true friends who care about you and accept you for who you are. Look for role models (people you can look up to). You may even want to get a mentor—someone older than you who can teach you, listen, give advice, and show you the way.

☑ **Think positive.** You have a good future ahead of you—and a lot to look forward to in life. If you make a mistake or mess up, tell yourself, "Everyone makes mistakes." Learn from your missteps and try again.

Chapter 5
The Body-Brain-Behavior Connection

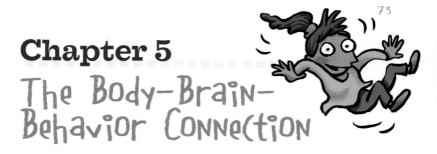

Your body works as a unit from head to toe, because all your parts are interconnected. You've probably heard of the mind-body connection: Your thoughts, which come from your brain, can affect how your body feels. And how your body *feels* can affect the way you think. It's like a **circle** going round and round.

Well, your behavior becomes part of the circle, too. Think about it: On days when you feel happy or excited, is your behavior better or worse than usual? Probably better. How about when you feel sad, upset, tired, or stressed out? Your behavior is probably worse—and that's completely understandable. The good news is there are things you can do to control the way this circle turns.

BOING!

Move That Body

You're reading a book right now, and that's a good thing. Reading feeds your mind. But reading is also a *sedentary* activity—that means you're sitting or lying down, and not moving your body much. (Turning pages takes hardly any energy.) Ask yourself: "How much of my day is spent on sedentary activities, like watching TV or DVDs, using the computer, or playing video games?"

Researchers at the Kaiser Family Foundation say that kids ages 8–18 are exposed to almost 11 hours of *media* each day (media is computer time, TV, movies, and music). For most kids, four of those media hours are television time. That's a lot of hours.

Doctors, parents, and experts of all kinds are concerned that kids today aren't getting enough exercise. In fact, government guidelines on raising healthy kids now recommend that school-age children (that's you) *should not be inactive for periods longer than two hours each day,* except when you're sleeping at night.

Have you been reading for a few hours? Okay, put the book down right now and move that body.

You can go outside and play sports, walk your dog, or toss a ball against a wall—anything to get moving. If the weather is bad and you want to stay inside, run up and down the stairs, jump rope, or throw yourself a dance party. Move, move, move.

The exercise you get each day can take all different forms. You exercise during gym, for example, and probably at recess, too. (If you stand on the sidelines and talk to your friends during recess, try to be more active instead.) Playing an after-school sport is great exercise because that means participation in games and practices. Or, maybe you take dance classes, work out at the YMCA or rec center, or do karate. You're probably active when you play outside too—bike riding, going to the park, playing tag, climbing on playground equipment, and all that fun stuff. These kinds of physical activities make you stronger, fitter, and healthier.

How much exercise do you need each day? The National Association for Sport and Physical Education (NASPE) says that school-age children should get **60 minutes or more** of physical activity per day. If you want to, you can break up the minutes. For example, you could do four sessions of activity for 15 minutes, or do two sessions lasting 30 minutes.

HELLO! What does this have to do with **behavior?**

Plenty.

Remember that body-brain-behavior connection? Well, exercising is a positive behavior that gives you positive results from head to toe. **When you're physically active, your body and brain are better able to handle mental or emotional challenges.** That's a mouthful! To put it simply:

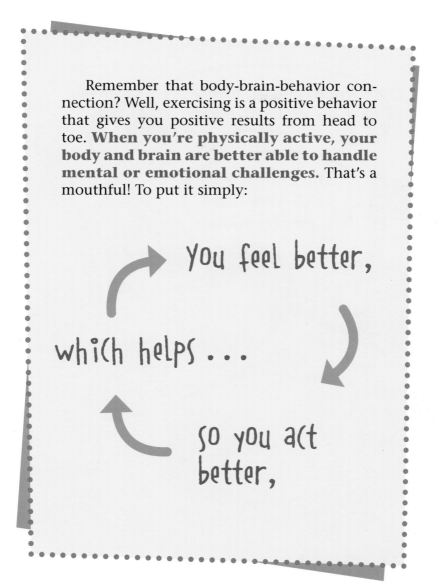

you feel better,

which helps . . .

so you act better,

Feed That Body

You're no dummy. You've learned a few things over the years about eating right, like it's a bad idea to gobble down nothing but super-sized fast-food meals and guzzle soft drinks all day. You even know that the green leafy stuff on your plate is called a vegetable.

You're getting older, and that means you're more in charge of what goes in your mouth. You might make your own breakfast each morning. You choose which snacks to eat after school. You may pack your own cold lunch or pick what you want in the cafeteria. Some nights, you might cook dinner for the family. So, you make choice after choice about what to eat.

Here's something big and important to remember:

* * * * * * * * * * * * * * * * * * *

The more nutrients you get each day, the BETTER YOUR BRAIN AND BODY wILL wORK.

* * * * * * * * * * * * * * * * * * *

So, what are **nutrients?** They're the parts of food that provide your body with the fuel it needs to run. That includes things like vitamins, minerals, proteins, complex carbohydrates, and *good* fats and oils. (Bad fats and oils are the ones found in chips, donuts, cookies, and cake.)

Choosing healthy foods is something your whole family can work on together. You can learn about the importance of:

- eating lots of fruits and veggies each day

- choosing healthy proteins (found in meat, eggs, and beans) and whole grains (found in whole-grain breads and cereals)

- avoiding too many packaged and "processed" foods (those with added chemicals)

- drinking lots of water to stay hydrated

- taking a daily multivitamin (one appropriate for your age)

Your family might choose to buy more *organic* foods—which means they're fresher and have fewer chemicals. Together, you might decide to eat fewer foods that are high in fats, sugars, and sodium.

When you eat better, you feel more balanced. Feeling more balanced improves your behavior. It's a win-win.

AN ADULT CAN HELP YOU HERE

If you want to learn more about how to eat healthy, you can check out a Web site like www.kidshealth.org, which talks about the U.S. Department of Agriculture's Food Guide Pyramid.

WARNING: TROUBLE AHEAD

You're at the age now when you're learning about the risks of smoking cigarettes, getting drunk, or getting high. Maybe you know kids who are using. Maybe you think this makes them seem older and more experienced—and you're getting curious about what it would be like to take up smoking or experiment with alcohol and drugs.

These behaviors won't make you seem older, and they definitely won't make you wiser. They *will* mess up your life.

If you're using chemicals—or you're *thinking* about using—talk to an adult you trust. Go to a parent, teacher, doctor, counselor, or some other adult who can help. You might start by saying: "I have something to tell you—something I'm really worried about sharing. But I know I need help." Be honest about what you've done and how often. Telling the truth about it is a big step in changing your ways.

Rest That Body

True story. There was a class full of students, listening intently to their very interesting teacher . . . when suddenly the weirdest sound arose from somewhere in the back of room:

pree-oo**ooh**, snuh, snuh, pree-ooooh, ooooooooooooh, SNUH, SNUH, pree-oooOH!!!

It was a sound unlike any the class had ever heard before. The students looked around curiously. The teacher craned his neck to see if a wild animal had somehow gotten in the room.

zZZZZ

Nope, it wasn't an animal—it was just Binky Higgenbottom.* He was sound asleep, snoring his head off (that explained the strange noises). A long line of drool connected his lips to his desk.

You see, Binky had a few problems at bedtime. He wanted to stay up late, watching funny talk shows and jumping on the bed. He liked to think of ways to s-t-r-e-t-c-h o-u-t his bedtime routine.

"Wait, I need a snack. I'm still hungry. More, please!

Gotta let Fido out. I should take a shower.

Um, I forgot to do some homework.

Gee, I'm so thirsty—better get a drink.

Do these pajamas look too small for me? Maybe I should change.

What's that noise? I heard a noise. Where's my nightlight?

Hey, look, there are some pretty cool dust bunnies under my bed—you've got to see this.

Wait, I still need to brush my teeth!"

On and on it went.

When Binky's alarm clock went beep-beep-beep in the morning, he felt like he'd been flattened by a bulldozer.

No wonder class time became naptime.

* His name has been changed to protect his privacy.

Don't be like Binky. It's embarrassing when the whole class sees you drooling or hears you mumble in your sleep. Plus, it hurts when you drift off and hit your head on the desk (CLuNK).

Make sure you get enough sleep each night so you feel alert and rested each day. How much sleep is enough? The National Sleep Foundation says kids ages 5–12 need 9–11 hours of sleep per night. Teens need 8½–9½ hours.

Not getting enough sleep night after night can lead to:

- Being irritable, hyper, or bad-tempered

- Decreased attention and short-term memory

- Poorer performance in school and after-school activities

Maybe you think it's unfair or stupid that the National Sleep Foundation says how much sleep kids need—and then announces those guidelines to parents. Shouldn't you be able to decide for *yourself?* Well, consider this:

When President Obama took office in 2009, his daughters—Malia and Sasha—got to move into the White House where there's a bowling alley, movie theater, and swimming pool. But the girls weren't allowed to stay up all night throwing gutter balls and calling up the chef for midnight snacks. Their bedtime was **eight o'clock.** The girls even had to set their own alarms and get themselves up for school, plus make their beds and clean their rooms.

Bedtime Basics

Try to set an early enough bedtime, especially on school nights, and then stick to it so your body gets used to a schedule. Wind down an hour beforehand by taking a bath or reading quietly in bed. Turn off all media during your wind-down hour—no more TV, computer, video games, or music—so your brain and body can settle down. Wake up at the same time each morning (this doesn't count on weekends, when everyone deserves a little extra shut-eye).

Check Your Engine

Think of your body as a vehicle—any kind you like. You're a monster truck, a cool sports car, a flashy convertible, a car that flies. No matter what kind of vehicle it is, it has an engine—that's what keeps it running.

Does your engine sometimes run too fast? Or too slow? How can you tell if your engine is at just the right speed for the "driving conditions" you face at different times during the day? You can use the chart on these pages to start paying more attention to how you feel and how this might affect your behavior.

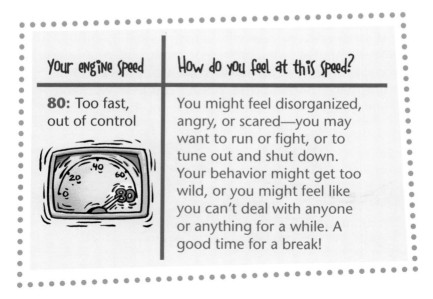

Your engine speed	How do you feel at this speed?
80: Too fast, out of control	You might feel disorganized, angry, or scared—you may want to run or fight, or to tune out and shut down. Your behavior might get too wild, or you might feel like you can't deal with anyone or anything for a while. A good time for a break!

Your engine speed	How do you feel at this speed?
60: High energy 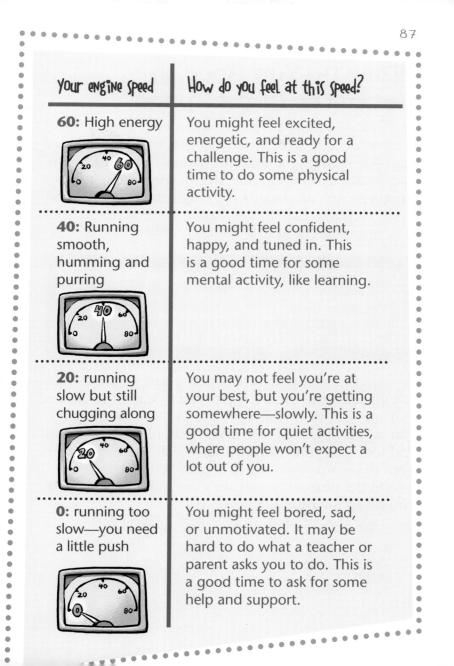	You might feel excited, energetic, and ready for a challenge. This is a good time to do some physical activity.
40: Running smooth, humming and purring	You might feel confident, happy, and tuned in. This is a good time for some mental activity, like learning.
20: running slow but still chugging along	You may not feel you're at your best, but you're getting somewhere—slowly. This is a good time for quiet activities, where people won't expect a lot out of you.
0: running too slow—you need a little push	You might feel bored, sad, or unmotivated. It may be hard to do what a teacher or parent asks you to do. This is a good time to ask for some help and support.

What Do You Need to Get to the Right Speed?

The day goes more smoothly when your engine speed is right on cue with what the situation demands of you. For example, you might be at a "60" just before gym class—perfect timing! By the time you head to Language Arts afterward, you might be at a "40" and ready to learn. Late in the day, sitting on the school bus, you might be at a "20"—no problems there.

> But if you're having some issues with your behavior, there's a good chance your engine is often out of control, out of rhythm, or out of gas.

What if you're at "20" when you get home from school, and your mom expects you to start your chores and homework? What if you're at "80" the moment you get to school, which makes it hard to settle down and focus on your work? At times like these, you may need to rev up your engine or slow it down.

On the next few pages are some quick ways to help you get in the right gear.

Move around a lot. Maybe you need to bounce, run, jog, spin, tumble, climb, or go for a bike ride. Besides keeping your body in good shape (see pages 74–77), exercise like this can help you burn off extra energy or cope with stress. Jump on a trampoline or an old couch (ask permission first), swim, play tug-of-war with friends, go to a park or playground, or if you have to stay indoors, climb up and down the stairs. Even *chores* can help you get physical: rake leaves, sweep the floor, or pull your little brother in a wagon.

Move around a little. If you're at school and it's not time for gym or recess (but you have the urge to move), stand up if you can. Take a restroom break so you can walk down the hall, or maybe get a drink of water. Some classrooms have ball chairs you can sit and gently bounce on, which can help, or sensory areas you can use during breaks (if you have permission). If moving around isn't possible, you could go out in the hall to briefly stretch your neck, shoulders, arms, and legs to get the kinks out.

Do "resistance work." Work your muscles through *resistance* by pushing your arms against a wall, pulling something (like a rolling backpack), carrying some heavy books around, jumping up and down for a while, hanging from the monkey bars, or rolling around in the grass. Try palm presses: Interlock your fingers and press your palms together, with your elbows up and out at shoulder level. Resistance activities can help your body feel more organized and get your engine numbers up or down, depending on what you need.

Find your rhythm. Rhythmic movement is relaxing and calming. You can dance, swing, lie in a hammock, rock in a rocking chair, or bounce on a workout ball.

Keep your hands busy. If you feel bored or fidgety, it helps to do something with your hands. For example, doodle, draw, or play with clay or a stress ball. If you need something that won't draw much attention, carry a straw, twist-tie, or paperclip in your pocket so you can pull it out and bend it in your hands.

Keep your mouth busy.
Sometimes, you might feel like you need to eat a crunchy food, suck on ice cubes or hard candies, or

chew something chewy. Doing something with your mouth can help your brain focus. At home, chomp on some sugarless bubblegum. At school, see if you can chew gum during times when you need to wake up or keep your mouth busy. Keep a water bottle at your desk, too.

Check your ears. Is there too much sound around you? If so, keep a pair of ear plugs handy. If you're in the car or on the bus, use headphones to tune people out. Sometimes, it helps to listen to soothing music so you can chill.

Create a calm place. Everyone needs somewhere private to go, even if that space is a closet, a homemade table-and-blankets fort, a pile of pillows, or a corner hideaway. Beanbag chairs are a great option because you can flop, crash, sit, or lie down on them.

Relax. Take a warm bath or hot shower. Take a nap. Get a hug from someone you love. Curl up with a good book. Turn off the overhead lights or put on a blindfold or eye-mask for a while. Ask a family member to give you a back massage, rub your feet, or tickle your back lightly. Snuggle up with your cat. Pet your dog. Watch the fish swim around and around in their tank.

Just Breathe

If you catch yourself zoning out in class or dozing off in the middle of your homework, get some oxygen to your brain—fast. It's as easy as breathing, because that's what you need to do: *breathe.*

Easy deep-breathing

This is so simple you can do it at your desk, and no one ever needs to know. Take a deep breath in for a count of five; blow it out, counting backwards from five. Breathe all the way down into your belly (instead of taking short, gasping breaths that go only as far as your chest). Do this at least five times. This type of breathing can help you wake up or calm down before a test.

Balloon breaths

If you need to relax and you have some room to spread out, you can try this breathing exercise. Sit on the floor, imagining you have a balloon in your belly. Inhale deeply for a count of five to fill the balloon with air. Now slowly let the air out of the balloon by counting backwards from five. Each time you do this, let your body flop to the ground, completely relaxed. Repeat several times. *Ahhhh . . .*

Relaxation and breathing combined

Read through all the steps before you give this one a try. Or, have a friend read them to you as you do the relaxation exercise.

1. Find a quiet place (if possible, do this outside because the fresh air feels great).

2. Lie down on the grass (or floor, if you're indoors) and get comfortable.

3. Close your eyes, but don't go to sleep.

4. Breathe deeply, focusing on your breath going in and out. Take your time.

5. When you feel calmer, continue breathing deeply, this time saying the word *relax* as you inhale and exhale.

6. Tense the muscles in your forehead as you inhale, then relax them as you exhale.

7. Next, do the same thing with the muscles in your jaw, then your neck, then your shoulders. Continue tensing and relaxing your muscles in time with your breathing, moving down your body to your arms, stomach, legs, and feet.

8. When you've reached your toes, tensing and relaxing them, take a rest. Keep breathing deeply.

9. Slowly open your eyes. You are now relaxed.

10. Enjoy this feeling!

"Fish out of water" exercise

If you need to get oxygen to your brain and you have some room to bend and stretch, try the Fish, a yoga position that gives you energy.

1. Lie on your back on the floor with your legs straight out, feet together. Place your arms on the floor, close to your body, palms down. Slide your arms under your body so your hands are hidden. (Fish don't have hands, get it?)

2. Now inhale a deep breath in, tilt your head back so the top of your head rests on the floor, and arch your chest slowly upward. Keep your weight on your elbows. Stay in this position, breathing deeply and exhaling, for about 30 seconds. (Try not to imagine yourself as a gasping fish—*that's* not relaxing!)

3. Slowly bring your head back to its original position and let your muscles relax. Hug your knees to your chest for a few minutes. Now you can get up, refreshed and ready to go.

Chapter 6
Mighty Motivators

You've come this far—way to go! Maybe you've made some changes in your behavior, and if so, you might have more confidence now. Remember all that talk about positive attention? (See pages 12–13.) It feels good when people notice what you're doing well. They *smile* more. That means *you* smile more. School goes smoother, and home is a nicer place to be when you have a feeling of:

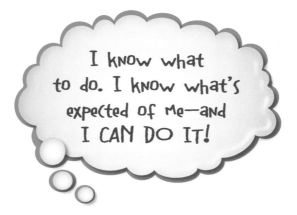

I know what to do. I know what's expected of me—and I CAN DO IT!

But life isn't some fairy tale where everyone lives happily ever after and dances down the street singing *tra-la-la*. You'll have good days and bad days, just like everyone else. Totally normal. Sometimes, you'll need ideas for motivating yourself; other times, you might want some extra help or support from adults. Read on for some ideas to help you on *those* kinds of days.

You Deserve a Reward

Most people respond well to rewards, whether they're adults or kids. For adults, a paycheck—the money earned for a job—is something to work hard for. (Just like you might work hard for an allowance.) Not every reward is about money, though. It's nice just to have someone say, "Hey, you're doing great!"

Parents like to hear things like "You're an awesome dad" or "Mom, you're the best" every once in a while. Teachers appreciate it when students say, "I'm learning a lot from you" or "That lesson was pretty cool." Those words are a reward for all the hard work parents and teachers do.

Think about what motivates *you*. Do you study a lot so you can make good grades? Do you do nice things for others because they say "thank you"? Do you take care of a pet because it shares love and affection with you? Do you play hard for the team so you win more games? Or do extra chores for extra cash? These are all rewards.

But rewards can be even more than money, compliments, and attention. It's *rewarding* to work hard on something you care about. That means you might feel proud of yourself or feel good that you helped someone else. Or you might gain a sense of accomplishment from a job well done.

So, some rewards come from *inside* you—like, "I'm happy that I'm working harder to get along with my family." Others may come from *outside* you—like allowance money or fun prizes.

When trying to improve your behavior, having REWARDS to look forward to can help motivate you. A reward (which can be small or big) is like **getting extra credit for things done right.**

AN ADULT CAN HELP YOU HERE

If you think rewards would be motivating, talk about this with an adult. Together, you can set up a chart that shows your progress in making behavior changes. (See page 109 for a sample chart you can use.) The rewards can come at different points along the way. Here are some ideas:

Fun Rewards

- Later bedtime (stay up 30 extra minutes)

- 30 extra minutes of computer, TV, or phone time

- Downloading three songs online

- 30 minutes of fun time with a parent

- Getting out of a chore for free today

- Picking one item from a grab bag (filled ahead of time with small things you like: trading cards, toys, hair accessories, bubblegum, pens/pencils, lip gloss, action figures, art supplies, and so on)

Fabulous Prizes

- Going to a movie

- Ordering pizza

- Going out for ice cream

- Choosing a special breakfast

- Getting a favorite treat in your school lunch

- Taking a quick trip somewhere fun (mall, park, library, rec center, YMCA)

- Choosing the menu for a meal

You can work your way to bigger rewards, too. If you've behaved well for a week or two and if you've accomplished each "I will . . ." on your list of goals, it may be time for an extra special treat. Here are some ideas:

Big-Time Bonuses

★ Rent or buy a new video game

★ Throw a party to celebrate reaching a goal

★ Invite friends and relatives for karaoke or dancing

★ Get new supplies for your favorite sport, hobby, or craft

★ Have some family fun: mini golf, water park, museum, skating rink, arcade

★ Go out for a meal at your favorite restaurant

★ Make a special dinner with all your favorite foods and dessert

★ Plan to visit a friend you don't often get to see, or have a sleepover

★ Buy what you've been saving your allowance for

★ Host an outdoor event for your friends: a softball or kickball game, badminton, water balloon fight, obstacle course, wacky races

★ Earn certificates for something special, like you get breakfast in bed (but you have to make these certificates ahead of time with a parent who can then let you choose one and reward you)

A Fancy Way to Track Your Progress

When you're working on your behavior at home or school, it helps to have a visual reminder—something you can *see* so you know how you're doing. A behavior chart is a simple tool that lets you track your progress each day. The "Put It in Writing" one on page 109 is a good start.

AN ADULT CAN HELP YOU HERE

Maybe you're already using some kind of a chart or points system at school, and if it's working for you, terrific! Stick with it. If you *don't* have any type of tracking tool, the one on the next page is useful. You just make a photocopy each week as you're working on your goals, and then fill in the chart every day. You can make two copies each week if you want one chart for school and one for home.

The chart includes space for up to three goals each week, but you can focus on only one or two goals if you'd like. Remember, make your goals *positive*—write down what you *will* do, instead of what you need to stop doing. Fill in the daily boxes with a star, checkmark, point, or smiley face.

Put It in Writing

My behavior goals for the week of _____

Goal 1: _____

_____

Sunday	Monday	**Tuesday**	Wednesday	Thursday	**Friday**	Saturday
☐	☐	☐	☐	☐	☐	☐

Goal 2: _____

_____

Sunday	Monday	**Tuesday**	Wednesday	Thursday	**Friday**	Saturday
☐	☐	☐	☐	☐	☐	☐

Goal 3: _____

_____

Sunday	Monday	**Tuesday**	Wednesday	Thursday	**Friday**	Saturday
☐	☐	☐	☐	☐	☐	☐

How I will be rewarded: _____

_____

Signed: _____

_____

(You and your adult helper can both sign here.)

Sign on the Dotted Line

Working on behavior is *work*. (But you knew that already.) It's not like you simply say, "I'm never, ever going to boss my friends again," and with a snap of your fingers—TA-DA!—you all live in perfect harmony forever. The work part still has to happen.

For some kids, changing a behavior is a slow process that requires lots of patient work—by kids *and* the adults who care for them. A behavior chart can be a part of that commitment. But sometimes more tools are needed.

A **Behavior Agreement** can be used at school, with the participation of your teacher and a parent. These types of agreements can help you follow rules more carefully or be less disruptive in class.

You, your parent(s), and your teacher will need to meet ahead of time, talk about your challenges, and put the Behavior Agreement into place. On page 112 is a sample Agreement that might work for your situation—or the school may already have an Agreement that has been used for students in the past.

The Agreement should say what you're expected to do and what happens if you *don't* do it. Will there be consequences? And if so, what kind?

The fun part is coming up with rewards—and *earning* them. How about:

★ Getting to be the teacher's helper?

★ Helping out in another classroom?

★ 10 minutes of a free-choice activity?

★ A free library period?

★ Reading with a buddy?

★ Being first in line for recess, for lunch, or at the end of the day?

★ Being a group leader?

★ Getting to tell a few jokes or to read aloud?

★ Taking care of the class pet?

Behavior Agreement

Date: _____

This is an agreement between

_____ (student) and

_____ (teacher).

Agreement

The student will do this: _____

_____

If the student does this, the teacher will give this
reward: _____

_____

If the student does not do this, the agreed
consequence will be: _____

_____

This contract is in effect as soon as it is signed. The
contract will be reviewed by the student and teacher
on this date: _____

Signatures

Student: _____

Teacher: _____

Any Questions?

With all this talk of charts and agreements, you may wonder:

Good question. The answer: Maybe you do, and maybe you don't.

You might be the kind of kid who can read about good and not-so-good behavior, and then figure out by yourself what to do—or you might *not* be.

You might be the kind of kid who likes tools (lists, charts, rewards) because they help you set up dependable routines—or you might *not* be.

You might be a kid who really needs extra structure and adult help—and that's okay, too.

Figure out what works for *you*. Maybe you'll need tools and supports for a short time, or maybe for longer while you're getting through a rough patch in your life. Give the tools a try—you won't know what works until you do.

A Few Last Words

Remember Cave Girl and Cave Boy (they got eaten on page 7). Yeah, that's sad. Not for the saber-toothed tiger, though—he was pretty happy about the whole thing.

Lucky for you, you'll never have to outrun a cranky prehistoric tiger. But you *will* have other challenges in your life, including figuring out how to make good choices about what you say and do every day. If ever you're in doubt about the "right" thing to do or say, think back to the Golden Rule. In case you've forgotten, here it is again:

Treat others the way YOU want to be treated.

That means friends, family (including sisters and brothers), relatives, classmates, other kids at school, teachers, neighbors, and even people you *don't* know.

Animals, too.

Here's a little something to add to the good-old Golden Rule: **Always remember to treat *yourself* well, too.**

A Note for Parents and Caregivers

As parents, we have the best job in the world. We get to watch our kids grow and change and reach for goals—and we grow, change, and reach right along with them. That's what makes parenting the *hardest* job in the world, too. Our role keeps changing, day to day. Plus, all the training happens on the job, which means we often learn by trial and error.

If your child is reading *Don't Behave Like You Live in a Cave,* chances are he or she has had problems with behavior. It may help you, as a parent or caregiver, to keep reminding yourself that kids don't choose to have behavior challenges (even if kids sometimes make bad choices). Your child may be struggling and in need of help—but he or she isn't "bad" or "impossible."

Throughout this book, I encourage kids to find an adult helper—someone they trust to help them notice any behavior challenges they're experiencing and figure out how to tackle them. This helper is probably *you.* You can read the book aloud with your child and try the suggestions together. Or you can simply let your child know, "I'm here for you if you have questions or need help."

A few helpful hints:

Stay positive. Believe in your child, and believe in yourself. Having a sense of "We can do this" makes the job easier and more rewarding.

Reach out. Talk to your child's teacher. Teachers are a fabulous resource; they know your child and want to help him or her succeed. Together, you and the teacher can brainstorm ways to make the school day a more positive experience. Help is also available in the form of other parents, doctors, counselors, books, Web sites, and more. In my role as a parent, there have been times when I needed expert help and I'm eternally grateful that I found it, because the advice and support I received was invaluable. Our family is stronger for it.

Offer praise. Take time to listen to yourself when you talk to your child. Are most of your statements positive and supportive? Avoid yelling, scolding, and nagging; instead, sincerely praise and encourage your child for what he or she is doing well.

Create structure. Kids need schedules and household systems they can count on so they know what to expect, and what's expected of them. Use tools like calendars, chore charts, and family meetings to keep things rolling smoothly.

Take care of you. At times you're tired and stressed, and you still have to make dinner, help with homework, and do everything else moms and dads do. Take time for yourself when you can. Breaks—even short ones—will help keep you sane. Find time to take a walk, breathe deeply, do yoga, talk to friends (about something other than the kids), or spend time on your hobby.

Have fun. If there's one thing kids need, it's your time and attention. Of course, you knew that already! But kids love it when they have your undivided attention for a certain amount of time per day, even a half hour or less, depending on what your schedule allows. Use that time to do what your child wants, whether that means playing on the playground, window shopping, doing arts and crafts, challenging each other to board games, or just talking. This one-on-one time will reaffirm how special your child is in your eyes.

Index

About the Author and Illustrator

Elizabeth Verdick was a perfect child who never once got in trouble. She's raising two perfect kids who will both grow up to be president someday. They have five perfect pets that never throw up on the carpet or eat weird stuff they fished out of the garbage.

Elizabeth has coauthored many books in the Laugh & Learn series, including *Dude, That's Rude! (Get Some Manners)* and *Siblings: You're Stuck with Each Other, So Stick Together.*

Steve Mark is a freelance illustrator and part-time puppeteer. He lives in Minnesota and is the father of three and the husband of one.

Steve has illustrated several books in the Laugh & Learn series, including *Dude, That's Rude!* and *Siblings.*

Free Spirit's Laugh & Learn™ Series

Solid information, a kid-centric point of view, and a sense of humor combine to make each book in our Laugh & Learn series an invaluable tool for getting through life's rough spots. For ages 8–13. *Softcover; 72–128 pp.; illust.; 5⅛" x 7"*